Sending Forth the Seed

For Kathie

Great sharing our Soul Collage
class together at Kat's studio.

May you love and laugh!

Judy Cox

2017

Sending Forth the Seed

Poems & Images
by Judy Cox

CENTER PLACE PUBLICATIONS

ISBN 978-O-9797581-O-2

Center Place Publications
Post Office Box 939
Crested Butte, Colorado 81224

www.NordicInnCB.com

Also by Judy Cox

A Pioneer Workshop
       Judy Slaughter Cole and Mary Mitchell Minturn
       First printing 1975
       Second printing 1979

In Sunshine and in Shadow
  Personal Portraits of ALS
  (Lou Gehrig's Disease)
       Judy Oliver
       First printing 1986
       Second printing 2001

"The Universe is what
you say it is, so say it."

James Burke

Table of Contents

Dedication ...

I dedicate this book
to my sweet mother
who at ninety loves to listen
to my poetry and is
unabashedly uncritical
of it all.

Mary Virginia Thomason

Judy and Ginny

Preface ...

by Judy Cox

I love this time in my life.

Some days I feel life is just starting, not in a slow way like growing up, but exponentially and day by day. Perhaps it is just all the time that has gone before, the building blocks, that make insights come faster now and thoughts reach so much further. I feel I truly live in a multiverse when in other eras my arena has been my backyard play spot, my routes to work and children's schools, my involvement in the community. When I think back, I have never wanted to be any age other than what I was. I have a great appreciation for the present.

So I give to you readers, especially my family and friends, this book of the creations of my life so far. I see far-reaching adventures ahead.

Foreword ...

by Marcie Telander

For most of her life Judy Cox has dreamt of a sanctuary, a cabin in the woods by a rushing stream that would be her "Center Place". From this still point she would put forth the seeds of her fertile experience and imagination. Here she would write, draw, paint, photograph and dwell. Here she would allow the spirits to move her, surrendering to her First Nature, that of a student, poet and ecstatic.

So, Judy sent up a voice. As it is with the true believer, Judy was able to invoke the cabin, the stream and the forest. Now, writing from that actualized Center Place she evokes the language of both the inner and outer wilderness. Through her poetry Judy brings us into an erotic realm of appreciation for the creatures and terrain just outside her cabin window.

Judy knows how to move slowly, speak slowly, allowing the sacred seed within each moment to materialize. To hone her attention she spent an entire season visually meditating and envisioning through the prisms of a kaleidoscope. The fragile, never repeated images from these contemplations have rendered new metaphors and sensations as fragile as butterfly wings, as eternal as a vision quest.

There is a sense of simple ceremony and reverence in many of Judy's poems. Within her nature and family-tribute poetry there is the awareness that writing is often an act of devotion and love. Captured in this is also the wisdom that if we love, we must also be willing to grieve.

Innocent, wise, humble, innately spiritual, witty and warm, Judy's poetry sets down roots, and gets the sap rising. As you read, expect balm for the soul and food for thought. All are a part of the earthy harvest carefully tended and gathered here.

Into the Middle Place

"In the midst of winter there is
an irrepressible summer."

Victor Frankl

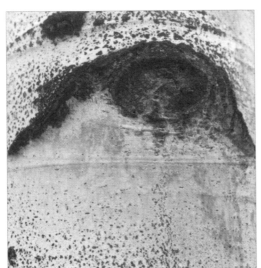
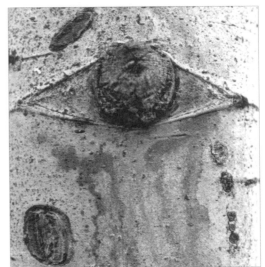

Eyes of the Forest

Her Mountain Guide

He knows her
>As that burst of energy
>Like stream droplets
>Colliding with rocks.

He remembers her
>From that sweet damp scent
>Home from hiking,
>Her sunburned hug.

He sees her
>In the crazy quilt
>Of blossoms
>That fill her arms.

>She is his surprise.

He teaches her.
>To see the eyes
>In an aspen forest.
>To mock wild drop-offs
>Land or sea.

He leads her
>To ask in expectation.
>Great things may come your way.
>And never exclude a soul.

But mostly he shows her how
>To laugh with joy
>Sending kindness all the way
>Into another's heart.

>He is her mountain guide.

Her Mountain Guide

For my husband, Allen

One Cup

Dawn Returns

As I gaze from my hilltop window,
Dawn breaks on the horizon
Turning the wintry gray lake and clouds
A warm peach.
Starlings still flit
Through silhouetted branches,
And the neighbor's dog
Follows the children to the school bus.
But my brother is dead.

That early morning
As we gathered in his kitchen
We held each other and sobbed tears
As our thoughts passed over
The tenderness and pain
Of the hours and days before.

Exhaustion, our limp bodies
Bent into old railback chairs,
Cigarettes, fresh donuts,
Third rounds of coffee
Cooling in mismatched mugs.

We had spent our energy
On a body and spirit
That we had each loved
In our own way.

Friend and lover
Sister and mother.
Our points of view
Like the angles of a hologram
Fused to mirror his image.
A life that simply changed its form
Continuing on.
We, too, continue on.

We who are letting go
Find strength
In the irresistible life force
Surrounding us,
In the return of dawn.

In memory of my brother,
Greyson Slaughter

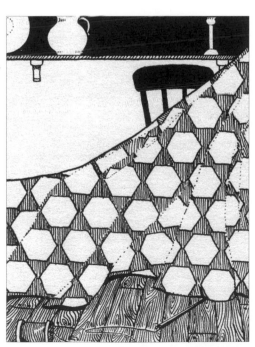

Illustration from
A Pioneer
Workshop

by Greyson Slaughter

Accept the Nourishment

Letting Go

My friend is letting go
Of brown spots
In her thinking.

Those little nagging spots
On zucchini
That flew up
To her attention
Blotting out
The brilliant waxy green
By the time
They arrived
As words on her lips
Saying,
"That vegetable
Is not suitable!"

Now
She'd like
To eat her words
And accept the nourishment.

For Judy Pauly

Blessings on the Wind

She holds
A glowing orb
Of energy
Between her palms,
And opening
Her hands
Lets go the balm.

It wafts in spirals
Upon the wind,
Its dharma spores
Connect within
All sentient beings,
Raining down
Through countryside
And town.

Her prayer flag
Keeps the vigil
In the holy night,
Surrounds her
With her blessings
And the Light.

For Corinne Cram

Before the Storm

The Family Album

1920's
Waist deep in golden wheat the sisters run
To catch their grandpa threshing in the field
Their laced boots fly, their hair reflects the sun.
Such rich historic memories pictures yield.

1940's
A little girl in Mary Janes and skirt
Looks toward grandpa's kodak, doll in hand.
Her mother in a tailored suit and shirt
Will drive with her on errands they have planned.

1970's
She sits in overalls in sister's arms
Leans on her shoulder, crimson-caped
And wearing page's hat with ostrich plumes.
She looks away just as the picture's snapped.

Generations pass along their genes,
But love passed down awakens children's dreams.

For Adrienne and Padget, my daughters

Mother and Judy, 1940's
by Herbert Slaughter

Adrienne and Padget, 1970's
by Marylou Schempf

The Birthday Pumpkin

A story for Carsten James Connolly
Born October 6, 1999

Daddy said, "I know somebody who is going to have a birthday." Carsten knew he was the one. Daddy wanted to make something for his little boy so they could have fun together. He thought of a great idea. "Let's make a birthday pumpkin." Carsten didn't know what that would be, but he watched Daddy cut out a circle and take off the top with the stem. Everything inside was orange and gooey and there were lots of white seeds. It smelled funny, too. Carsten's job was to scoop all of it out with a big spoon. When he was done, it was empty inside. Daddy started carving the outside with his sharp knife.

What would it look like? It wasn't eyes and a smiley mouth with teeth. It was Carsten's cake with candles! There was not another pumpkin in the whole world like his. Then Daddy said, "Let's light the candles." So they lit one candle inside the pumpkin and turned out the lights in the room. All of a sudden all three candles on Carsten's birthday cake lit up!

That night Carsten fell asleep in his bed watching his bright birthday candles. His daddy fell asleep remembering how happy he was the day his little boy was born three years before.

Sunshine and Shadow

Waking to a Southern Morning

Half seen outside the louvered window,
    A chartreuse flutter of
    Bamboo fronds
    Making shadow patterns
    Across my bedroom wall.

Past these silhouetted stalks
    A layer of speckled violet,
    Then limbs of black against
    An azure blue.

Bees weave and drone
    Determined on their flight
    Through pastel throats
    Turned sunward.

And I say,
    Come shimmering light,
    Come dove song
    I open my shutters
    To your morning call.

For Padget and John Hartung,
my daughter and son-in-law

"Joy is the leap of the sun
Hurtling upward from the drowsy dark.
'Alleluja' the path sings.
Do you hear it?"

Collette Inez

Leap of the Sun

My Quiet Farewell

Yes, it's time.
This is the day to walk alone
In the fields and woods
And by the lake.
I have put it off
Not wanting its coming
Ignoring the box
Under the table
Then back on a closet shelf.

Spring is here.
It's past the point
Of buds and chartreuse leaves.
The seeds from last year's
Zinnia blooms
Are sprouting in rows.

And the martins have returned.
How I had wished
He were here then
To tell me how to prepare
For the appointed day,
When to open the doors,
How to avoid the sparrows.

The box, the funnel, the scoop,
The plastic bag
And typed label
Cremains: James Thomas Oliver.
They strike me
As a still-life
On the floor.
I take a picture
Wondering
What I will ever do with it.

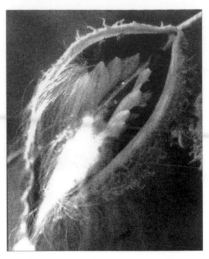

Sending Forth the Seed
Photo first published in In Sunshine and in
Shadow: Personal Portraits of A. L. S.

When I filled the velvet bags
For friends and family,
I used the scoop and funnel.
I cried at the first touch
Of the scoop
To the ashes.

They're not like ashes, though,
But rather pieces of shell
Mostly white.
In those last days
We talked about his shell.
That's all it was.
He was such shining beauty inside.
But when they came
To take the shell away
That late afternoon,
I mourned for it
Because I loved it, too.

I gather up the plastic bag.
Quite a lot of ashes
Left for me.
I'm doing what he asked.
He wrote a message which ended:
"Bury some in your flower beds,
Under our trees,
Then scatter some down at the dock,
In the lake,
And just as you go along
On walks in the woods."

I climb the hill
To the meadow
And look across its openness
To the big maple
Remembering a fall day
When I lay beneath its branches
Watching monarchs meander south.

I dip my hand in.
The touch!
It's so immediate
My senses are flooded.
"Do this in remembrance of me."
The bits of wafer
On a communion tray.
My love's body.

Yet, I choose the places.
Purple wildflowers here
A young tree there.
I pass through a narrow opening
In the hedge
Into a wide place
Thinking how he
Passed from this life to the next
As I held his hand.

I toss some ashes in the bordering woods
In memory of our snowy
Cross-country walks.
Our dog runs up ahead
On the path
Looking back as if to say,
"Don't wander!"
She was just born
The summer I first loved him.

I've saved the rest
For the water.
As the ashes slide from my palm,
I now see clearly
The body's density.
The larger pieces
Drift quickly down
But the dust swirls
In a lingering cloud
Near the surface.

The material
And the spirit
Separated mercifully
In death.

In memory of my husband,
James Thomas Oliver

Into the Light
Photo first published in In Sunshine and in
Shadow: Personal Portraits of A. L. S.

This poem was published in the University of Kansas' literary
journal, Kansas Quarterly in 1991 and received the Seaton
Honorable Mention Award.

Now and Then

The bed table,
    A receptacle for
    The calendar of the month
    The activities of the day
    The menu for lunch
    A plastic pill cup
    And used juice glass.

Across the room,
    The azalea needing water
    The candy box
    Half full of chocolates
    Half with crumpled fluted papers,
    A little handmade quilt
    Over the wheelchair arm.

On the walls,
    Photos of horseback riding
    Fly fishing, and jeeping
    A grandchild's graduation
    The family home and garden
    A husband's distant smile.

Now and Then.

The Cottonwoods

A soft breeze
From heaven
And the North
Caresses the cottonwoods,
Lifts their filmy puffs
Of seeds
Into the air
And sends them
To us,   They descend
We who need   From overhead,
The comfort   Alight gently
Of their softness. On our mourning forms
                  And brush the tops
                  Of granite
                  Etched with family names.

                  They cover the earth
                  We shovel
                  In farewell.
                  A comforter of down
                  For the one
                  We lay to rest.

For Betty Light
at Mason's burial

Hal's Fence

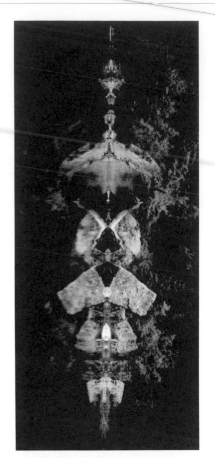

*Lizard Lake
Reflection*

Into the Middle Place

I am in cave space
Slipping slowly under
Still water which rises
From the hot eye of the earth.

Silence and sage pure aromas
As ancestors' toes slide
Close to mine.
A *pavant*
Shared by all tribes,
The middle place of the heart.

I see my grandfather's hand
Reaching down to me
In the moist travertine rock,
His fingers and knuckles,
His beautiful bones
Full of remembrances
Of love between us.

The hand that reached for me
In rescue from the clothesline pole.
The hand holding the fan of cards
As we played canasta.
These old fingers embrace
My tender hand leading me
Into my own heart ...

With the same ancient wisdom
Of all my grandfathers
Who walked on
The crust of our Mother
And bathed in her mystical waters.

In memory of my grandfather, Gamp
Herbert Franklin Slaughter

"Befriend instinct.
Tend the invisible garden."

K. Finn

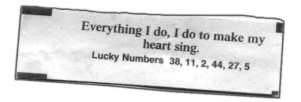

Everything I do, I do to make my
heart sing.
Lucky Numbers 38, 11, 2, 44, 27, 5

Fifty-Five Word Story

This story was created for a very short story contest designed by John Napier in Crested Butte.

The daughter broke open the anticipated fortune cookie after sharing a Chinese meal with her mother. "Everything I do, I do to make my heart sing." Yes! So appropriate for both. The daughter honored her aging mother with an engraved brick in the gloriously blooming Garden of Remembrance. Both cherish the words: "Her heart sings."

*For the caregivers at the Gunnison Living Community
and the volunteers for Hospice*

Kansas Sunflowers

Kaleidoscope Scenes

I found myself some years ago irresistibly drawn to a kaleidoscope with designs formed by brilliant colors and shapes of iridescent glass pieces tumbling amidst gold beads. I have delighted in it since then and have written this series of poems while gazing into the illuminated viewing tube.

As I let myself become immersed in its world, I open to new dimensions and let the kaleidoscope speak to me. My attitude is one of wonder and child-like joy in the experience of seeing infinite newness in each image. I am often surprised by my interpretations of the changing designs and find their meaning clarified at later times.

I thank Thomas and Carol Paretti for crafting this unique kaleidoscope titled "Starfield."

Pale Pentagon House

Pale pentagon house
A star overhead.
Light beams infuse
Its center with red.

Glyphs overlaying
An ancient starfield.
Magentas and citrons
Tumble and reel.

Pears in a basket
Of lavender bands.
Sand dollars lie
Beneath jellyfish strands.

A wayfarer signals
The return of the whale
And wine-winged angels
Let go of the sail.

Anna's Place

Moth Eyes and Butterfly Wings

Moth eyes
And butterfly wings,
Turquoise of damsels
And celadon rings.

Gold-shafted spears,
Where could they land?
They meld into stars
On the back of a hand.

Lavender twists
And jeweled pinnacles,
Seed center of petals
And citronesque tentacles.

Panels of fuchsia
Behind silver-hued spires,
Pearlized sequins
And criss-crossing wires.

Black starfield so elegant,
Flames in the sky.
Shadows on sundials
Hurtling by.

Butterfly Wings

Nature's Mosaic

What's Getting In?

What's getting in
Through the holes
In the screens?
Crystalline structures
On katydid wings.

Bones opalescent
Peach bodies of sponge.
Boom-a-rangs hurl
And ghost forms lunge.

A "W" spreads out
In elongated scallops,
And through tendrils and vines
A black horse gallops.

Lavender dolphins
In lime green crowns
Leave chrysanthemum gifts
At the entrance of town.

The emerald spring coils,
The lattice is broken,
Starfields rush in
When the portals are opened.

Whorled Yellow-ridged Shells

Where have you come from
Whorled yellow-ridged shells?
From gold specks in the night
And Tibetan-pure bells.

Black buffalo skulls
With peregrine feathers.
Winds from the starfields
Through aspens and leathers.

"Break with the mundane."
Say fire letters in script.
Follow the one line
To the doves on the cliff.

Triangles spread out
And pyramids form.
Snow crystals fall
Where oceans are warm.

Circling fireflies
Tire from their flight.
Sea life is restless
And land mammals fight.

Riding Brave

Favorite Outhouse

Motionless Windmills

Motionless windmills
Atop double-walled towers,
Their filigreed blades
Are stillbirthing power.

Pink petaled flowers
Encased in ice,
A blue garden wall
Encircles them twice.

Beaks of hummingbirds
Penetrate boulders
As gold ore flows out
In myriad odors.

The star of Osiris
Beams laser-gold lines
To a tentacled starfish,
Its mirror in the brine.

We're inside of a jewel box
Staring toward space
When an image returns
Of our wondrous face.

Cave Symbol of Sun

Cave symbol of sun
With its rays extending
To far-reaching walls
With light unending.

The black rose of night
Sprouts from gold beads of sand.
Wild spinning and prancing
Of the headdress of man.

Why do they gather,
These four swords of light?
To anchor the ancients,
To tether the kite.

Pincers are narrowing,
Citron hearts spread.
Webs spun in twilight,
Jeweled skins are shed.

Pods of the lily,
Seeds rattle inside.
Primordial ooze
Where the answers lie.

Letter Openers

Breast Shields of Fuchsia

Breast shields of fuchsia
With studs made of gold,
Shadows surround them.
Sheep leave the fold.

Cloven-hooved creatures
Tread paths in the sand.
Through thorn vines and tendrils
Tribes roam the lands.

Dimensions unfold
With peculiar ease.
Turquoise crustaceans
Lift up on a breeze.

Horns full of plenty
Are battery-lit.
Jesters in green tights
Fumble and slip.

Where is the solace
Of Calm Abiding?
Black petals of night
With seed center hiding.

*"Your ability to create
ends where fear begins."*

Barbara Marciniak

High Mountain Sheep

Paper Crane Kite

A Raven Descends

A raven descends
In a crimson red star
From the black hole in space
Where all answers are.

Prayers carried on sage smoke
Drift up to his knowing.
He flies with their essence,
Winds shimmering, blowing.

A raven encircled
By gold light of dusk
Flies back to the circle
With conundrums for us.

Watch for pearlized wings
Of ascending blue cranes
Trailing ribbons of violet
Through gathering rains.

Veins on a leaf
Like lifelines in hands,
Crystals in envelopes
Mailed to all lands.

Namasté

"I honor the place in you
in which the entire Universe dwells.
I honor the place in you
which is of love, of truth,
of light and of peace.
When you are in that place in you,
and I am in that place in me,
we are one."

Egg of Life

Sacred Geometry

Ten Stones Are Standing

Ten stones are standing
Opalescent at night.
They draw through their portal
A rush of black light.

Magenta-fringed banners
Swoosh with the flow
As a globe of light rises
In a phosphorous glow.

The table is set,
Sterling knives in a line.
Guests take their places
While mongrels whine.

Arrows point within.
Sand fills the spaces.
Silence descends
And covers pale faces.

Stone walls are hung
With rich brocade tapestry.
Heart chambers are clogged
With words and complexity.

Beads on Silk Ribbons

Waiting for Summer

Beads on silk ribbons
And clovers in chains,
We swing in the hammock
And wait for the rains.

Five scissor-winged swallows
With lavender legs
Fly to the steeple
Through a mist-laden haze.

Stars streak through the heavens
And splash in the sea.
Fishermen navigate
Cautiously.

A red spirit line
On a land turtle's back
Points to the ancients
Who have traveled this path.

What are the answers
Transmitted to us?
Inhabit the tulips.
Impregnate the dust.

A Fallen Black Star

A fallen black star
Is splayed out on the earth,
Tied down with red ribbons
On each point 'round its girth.

White wings encircle
The space overhead.
Turquoise-tinged egrets
Leave offerings of bread.

Purple glyph out of Asia
Floats in mid-air.
Eyes focus in wonder
Asking why it is there.

The glyph mutates
While watched
Into half circles
And dots.

It spreads out
From its center
So all answers
May enter.

Bark Abstract

Feathers Brushed Gold

Feathers brushed gold
Dipped in rose colored ink
Words of creation
Deep magenta to pink

Spring nodules are budding
'Round a center that's fixed,
A profusion of blossoms
With all colors mixed.

A sunflower mandala
With cords of chartreuse
Draws to its center
Clear joy for our use.

Antennae spread out
Attracting the light
To our blue marble planet
In the gold spangled night.

This radiant light
Glows from our being
As we twirl through space
In a dance of all-seeing.

Clear Joy

"Imagination
is evidence
of the Divine."

William Blake

Past the Edges

"If you hear a voice within you saying
'you are not a painter,' then by all means paint
... and that voice will be silenced."

Vincent van Gogh

Sage

Li-wu

My friend and I
Sipped green tea
In the shadow
Of a black horse
From a Chinese tomb.

We spoke from our depths
Of that which
Gives us life,
Of the circumstances
Given to us
And ones we've made.

As always
We had no feel for time.
An energy greater than us
Hovered
Over the chopsticks
And rice.

Then fortune intervened.
We cracked
Our folded wafers
And slips of paper
Intruded on our clarity.

How could a fortune
Be phrased as a question?
Is not the prediction
Of our destiny
A statement?

Yes!
Mine read:
"Your life will be happy and peaceful."
Quite satisfactory
And as expected.

But my friend's read:
"What makes an apple
Fall to the ground?"
I wanted to say
To the paper
"You tell me!"
This is not right.

I'm puzzled
And wonder,
What does make an apple fall?
At first
I thought it was gravity.
All too obvious.
Then I thought
Of the wind, the ice and fire.
All possibilities.

But what if
The green apple
Rotted
And let go?
All so natural
And in its own time.

Still pondering
I turn the papers over.
Her "Learn Chinese" word is
Green, lu-se
Mine
Gift, li-wu

For Ann Hyde

Pristine Point

The Thousand Sparkles

You are the thousand sparkles
Dancing in unison on the water.
You are joy and energy
Singing with the sun.
You burst forth at daybreak
From behind the far hill
In a moment of "Aha!
I see, I understand."

You are the dawn,
The light-bearer,
The light-scatterer.
You fling your rays
Far and wide like seed
Blowing in the wind
And falling in every field.

This Face

This poem is a result of a writing exercise with friends in which we each drew
four words and wrote a spontaneous poem using each word. My words were:
torment, woven, noise, move.

A rush of breath
Of breeze
A pounding heart
The trees
A noise
A tenuous hand
Moves
Toward the glass,
Draws
The woven drapes
Aside.

The face
That looms
That glowers,
Threatens
In the gloom!
Same countenance
That always
Fills that room.
The torment
Cannot be
Let go,
Faced with
This face
She knows
She knows.

Lupine

Poetry Night

You kicked the chameleon,
Hurled the lizard
With your words.

Mountains turned crimson
And danced in the river valley.
I was there.

I've been in that place before
Shocked by the splash
From the frost pond
And the startling blue above.

You made me remember.

For David Moore

Ancient Memory

Free Form

I Am

I am the horse
Black, shining
Shaking its mane
Loosing its ropes
Rearing up, hooves high
Seen against the mountain
Whetstone, new snow.

This horse's prayer
Is not supplication,
But exclamation!
Times to come,
Pounding hooves
Over all impediments.

Rising like Pegasus
To the stars
And beyond
FREE.

Wild

Wild sounds
In the early morning air
Rivet me
To my dark window
Searching for clues.

Eioooo, yip yip yip yip
Comes from the
Mountain's base
With answering howls
From the opposite meadow.

Anxious barks
Of domestic dogs
Join the chorus.
I, too, am enlivened
By the boisterous pack
At the end
Of the night's hunt.

But like a dog
Behind doors
The cold glass,
So tauntingly clear,
Separates me
From this dark outside.

Sometimes coyotes
Lure dogs away
From the indoor warmth
Of food and owners.
Dogs catch the scent,
The raucous wildness
Of their ancient cousins.

My insides are stirred.
How would it be
To have wild blood,
Blood to loose
My uncivilized self,

To hone my senses
To survive,
To howl
With blatant joy
At daybreak?

by Liz Eflin

This painting is a gift from Liz Eflin in
response to the writing of "Wild."

Dalai Lama

Standing on the Dark Road to the Cloud Forest

Have not the stars above
Descended
Becoming fireflies?

Is not the undulating trill
Of the night forest
My own vibration?

The wind
Reaches a crescendo
And my spirit
Is swept with joy.

I was in Costa Rica in 1989 at a conference called "Seeking the True Meaning of Peace" when I wrote these poems. It was my great privilege at that time to spend informal time with the Dalai Lama and Dyhani Ywahoo, a Cherokee spiritual leader.

In the Mist

Translucent purple
Dripping, bending in the breeze
Dark buds opening.

Dyhani Ywahoo

My Beloved Monks

My beloved monks
Are inside me
Melting me gently
With their om.

Oming my heart
Into liquid gold
Drops into puddles,
Circles colliding,
Rings flowing
Outward, outward
From the center place.

I am the one line,
The one tone
That has no opposite.
I am the lone prayer flag
Anchored in the rocks
Fluttering.

My prayers
Ride on the high winds
Above the clouds,
One, one, one
Everywhere
The circle goes.

For Judy Theis

A plate created by my sister,
Janet Crawley

"All good things from the Center Place."

I di wana an kwa'jol a'kokshi

Zuni saying

The Center Place

Washed by the Stream

The Massage

Let it flow
Let it melt and pour out
Like spring snow from roof gutters.

Let my senses retreat
From drawn rose drapes
Across Victorian windows.

I am warm, still, and waiting
With a prayer to myself to
Let it go.

It - the ice dams of the winter,
The barriers I've subtly constructed
But rarely noted.
The particles, leaves and twigs
Washed to the stream
When they can cling no longer.

Let me be here now,
Vulnerable to the first
Scent of the oil
Touch of a hand
Following the muscles
Finessing the knots.

I feel the rain and wind
On ancient canyon walls
Eroding sand
Then chunks and boulders.

Melodies, fingers on guitar strings
Mimicking those
Serenading my back.
Wild iris citrus oil on
Eyelids and cheekbones.

Let me not resist the pressure
On a tender spot.
Let me bare
My most aware
And honest center.

May the rose mist
Alerting my skin as it settles
Alert me before I
Hold back and hold on,
Before the leaves and twigs
In spring eddies
Can build dams in fallen logs.

For Jennifer Rose

This Way

My Ancient Memory

My ancient memory
Is alive!
Instead of languishing
And drooping
Where it's tied,
It flutters
In the breeze
Then flies.

It nearly shouts to me
To see
Its hand-drawn symbol
Eye to eye,
Remembering my plea
To bring my knowing
Back to me.

Bear Tree   *Three Old Friends*

After Discovering My Energy Field Is Not as Clear as I Thought

I want to open myself up.
Way up.
Like my insides
Are the universe
And instead of being
A pretty twilight blue
With little stars floating in it,
It's a can of worms!

But the can has to be opened,
Not in a pretty way,
But sawed open, jagged,
With that old-fashioned
Primitive sort of opener
That is rusted,
That you only take
On an occasional camping trip,
That you would never
Keep in a drawer upstairs
In your nice kitchen.

After all, my insides
Are the universe for me
And I'm the one
With the can opener.

I want to stare
Right at those maggots,
See them
For what they are.
I want to know
They are there.

Why did I ever think
They were so powerful
I had to can them,
Hide them,
Preserve them?

They've invaded my universe
And I've been left
With a thin edge of skin
That the sun shines on.
And I think everything is O.K..

I'm pretty and cheerful,
I dance around and play.
It's a sham.
It's a shame.
My tender child
Frightened into believing
I must hide my spirit
To be pleasing to others,
Taking to heart
All those worms
Of admonition
Long after my mother cares.

I shake that rusted can
And maggots burst forth
Into the light.
I watch them sprout wings
And fly far away from me.

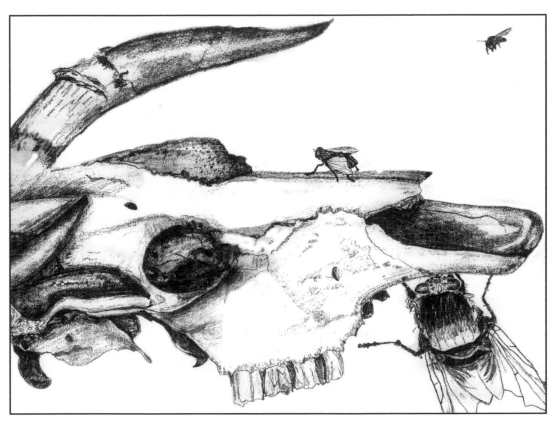

Metamorphosis

Just Pie in the Sky

Carol's Horse

"When you learn, teach. When you get, give."

Maya Angelou

Just Pie in the Sky

It's a bad day at the office
In the high rise L.A. tower.
The big exec clicks off his screen.
His attitude is sour.

Picking up the Journal
To keep up on breaking news,
His eye falls on a single ad
And he begins to muse...

"Colorado acreage"
And riverfront at that.
Mountains, aspen all around
And a cowboy in a hat.

Sounds so good he wastes no time.
His secretary's summoned.
"Get this realtor on the line.
Here's her 800 number."

As he waits to hear the info
He slips into a dream.
He himself is on a horse
Where the air is crisp and clean.

His wife no longer shops the malls
And plans their social whirl.
She tends the ranch house, bakes the beans,
A wholesome western girl.

His kids have stopped their whining
About their constant need
For videos, designer clothes.
Now they like to read.

He has time to pen some verse
Like the poet Baxter Black.
He writes of spring thaws and summer rains
And an old hay rack.

Then suddenly he's startled
Into stark reality.
The little ranch he's pictured
Must be purchased for a fee!

Thirty acres of this land
Will cost him 2 plus mil.
His stomach takes a nose dive.
He reaches for a pill.

The realtor wants to hear from him.
She's outlined all amenities.
He's not real interested now
And utters some profanities.

His lazy dream's in smithereens.
He can't shed this faster track.
So to his secretary he replies,
"That's no. Just fax-her-back."

And that rhyme's the closest he ever got
to the name of Baxter Black.

JUDY,

    THANX FOR THE KIND WORDS.   IM LGAD YOU
LIKE MY STUFF.
    MY COMPLIMENTS ON SUCH A GREAT RHYME!
ITS KINDA LIKE RHYIMING ORANGE, I THINK.

I DID EACENTLY RHYME SHRAPNEL WITH
"SHIP CAP"NL.
    MY FAVORITE IS OGDEN NASH.
HE RHYMED LOS ANGELES WITH TARANTULAS!

    take care DARLIN AN THANX FOR BRIGHTIN
MYD AY.

                 baxter

Forgotten Wheel

Haven in the Woods

Bob Goes Fishing
Written for an anonymous friend

A dude, who just arrived in the county, builds a house, settles in and meets his neighbor. He mentions he's tried a few fishing spots but hasn't had much luck. Taking pity on him, the neighbor suggests they meet the next evening after dinner. Somewhat surprised by the timing, but interested in the prospect of fishing with a local, he agrees and asks what he should bring along. "Don't need a thing," his friend replies. That means, he guesses, not even the fly-fishing wardrobe and equipment he had invested in.

They meet as it is getting dark and instead of heading up the valley, he follows his new friend to the curb where water is rushing through a ditch supplying the neighborhood with stream water. He's handed a flash-light and told to beam it on the ditch. The object is to scoop the salmon onto the lawn. Bob goes with the program. Seems that the locals have done this before. "Fishing" was a little slow until Bob started rattling and kicking the culvert pipe. This flustered the shy fish into swimming downstream. Those he could not scoop fast enough were scooped at the other end of the yard.

All in all it was a good night's catch. Bob was proud of himself for his culvert-stomping technique, a new insight which he was glad to bring to his adopted community. He had mastered salmon fishing in thirty minutes, and as he carried home his trash bag of fish he realized he had become a local.

Finding My Nature Diva

I am swinging

When I notice her.
The head and winged body
Emerging from cloud strands
Trailing behind her
Like ribbons of energy.

I lay in the grass

As she grows big curly hair
And smells a rose.
An eye forms
Winking at me.

I stand shading my eyes

As she shape-shifts
Into Pegasus
Galloping out of the clouds
And up my forest road.

For Geoff and Christine Rollert

Another Shape-Shifter

The Ballad of Mike the Headless Chicken

The story that you're about to hear
Is absolutely true,
Not told by the *Enquirer*
Or the likes of such a crew.

The Denver Post, an upright rag,
Retold this tale last May,
But *Life* and *Time* before it
Had given it some play.

It's of Mike, the headless chicken
Whose disability
Did not impair his barnyard strut
Or harm agility.

Preparing for a Sunday lunch
Back in 1945,
His owner lopped his head off,
Then stared in rapt surprise

As the rooster wobbled from the block,
Picked up where he left off.
He tried to peck, preen, even crow,
But just let out a cough.

You see, the farmer placed the ax
To leave on most the neck,
His mother's favorite piece of meat,
So he did it - what the heck?

But because he left the brainstem
There was no handicap!
The wily farmer saw he had
A resource he could tap.

He dropped Mike's gruel straight in his gullet
To see how long he'd last.
He packed him off to scientists
Who stood aside aghast.

So he took the chicken on the road,
His head in alcohol.
The farmer made a tidy sum.
And the chicken had a ball.

He toured with a two-headed calf
And garnered fame galore.
He outlived all his barnyard mates.
In fact, he died at four.

And now there is a festival,
All the chicken you can eat,
An egg toss, lots of stupid jokes
And music with a beat.

Mike, the Headless Chicken Day
A 5-K run, at that.
Come run and get your T-shirt
And some droppings on your hat!

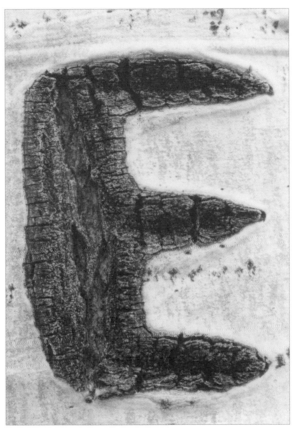

E for Everything Good

Still Life

Polliwogs

Now there's a word
I won't be using
Anytime soon.

I'll just toss it
In the trash
Making room
For more useful words.

Economize, I tell myself,
It's time to tighten up.

"I choose to live ... so that which came to me as seed,

goes to the next as blossom

and that which came to me as blossom, goes on as fruit."

Dawna Markova

Abundance

Serenity

"If a grail appears, the soul must follow."

William Least Heat Moon

The Woodsman

This poem is the co-creation of those who attended an evening of poetry in a lovely garden along the East River. Each person contributed a line without seeing what others wrote. Marcie Telander arranged the lines in this delightful verse.

I contributed the last three lines of the first verse which led me to draw the woodsman in an old tree stump.

Moonlight

Moonlight, quiet, peace, calm—
we hold our fruit, watching the aspens,
running from the biting,
hungry flies.
And then, on night black wings of
the fleeing crow
the Woodsman parts
dripping branches and peers into
the cabin window.

We sit on the couch,
in the iridescent light
of a flickering candle,
of sunset,
sweetly singing
a reverent goodbye.
Outside, the bear raises up and demands
the lid of the dumpster be opened.

"Mitakuoyasin! For all my relations!" sings the irreverent troll.

For Mackenzie Chernushin

Llama Rider

There once was a girl who rode llamas.
She preferred to ride in pajamas.
But she dressed *them* in bows
And elegant clothes
And the babies would follow their mamas.

For Adrienne Taylor

Look for a lovely thing

and you will find it

"God provides the first line of a couplet

The poet must seek out the second."

Anthony Hecht

Translation of ancient poem-modern lingo

She Walks Our Valley

"There is a loneliness in two-leggeds separated from nature."

Marcie Telander

Between the Worlds

The Sentinel

Sentinel on the pole top
Black, red spirit paint
Splashed on each wing.
Yah she toe waa!

The high view
Seeing out, down and up.
Morning mountain mist
Hovers over
Still pond water
Beneath his perch.

Does he watch the far peak
Or the trout
Beneath the surface?
Does he know
What's yet to be
In the mist
Between the worlds?

For Sho'ena Harris and Joseph Glosemeyer

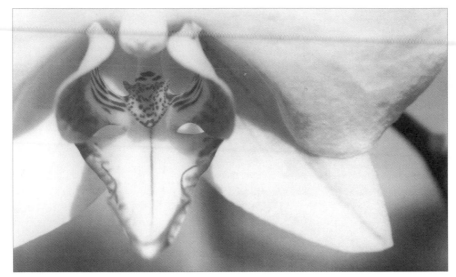

Orchid Mask

Inside the Heart

We pass by many people
In our lives
Like so many flowers
In a garden.

How rarely we stop
To see the beauty
Inside a single heart.

Vibration of Lavender

As I stand amidst the fields
Of St. Marie,
Bells toll
In distant chartreuse hills
And I breathe in the scent of dusk.

What birds sing here
In this vibration of lavender?
Whose silver scissors
Slice stems heavy with blossoms?

I melt into reverie
Bees buzzing
To cadenced music.

For Susan Marrion

Kalanchoe

She Walks Our Valley

There is a time
As Dawn
Walks up our valley
When the blue-gray
Of the sky
Matches
The blue-gray
Of the snow.

Now is this time.

Silhouettes of aspen
Frozen as the snow,
Branches
Laced across the sky,
Trunks,
Thin lines
Against the white.

Dawn's cape
Trails pale pink
Tinting Whetstone Peak.

She pauses at our stones
Not wishing to disturb
The circle of coyote tracks.

Laced with Snow

Remnants

Past the rock-walled garden
Still lying fallow
And cedars
On the canyon rim,
I descend
By switching back
Watching for the river's bend.

I smell spring's imminence
In a cool, moist breeze
Yet what I see
Are hollow forms of life
Left by winter's freeze.

Whorled stalks of reeds
Brittle, delicate,
Bleached pale pearl-grey,
Yet within them
memories of summer green
Caught in a last sun ray.

It makes me think:
Is beauty found
Just in the prime
Or does it still reside
In the form and symmetry
Of what is left behind?

And the river,
It flows through it all.
Ancient, all-seeing
Watercress and crackling ice
Its being.

My eye is drawn
To a sunny glade
And veering from the path
I find remains.
Whitened, even mossy bones
Attest to final pain.
The jawbone of a deer
And vertebrae
Spread down the lane.

Did she charge
To keep her young
From being prey?
Did she die of hunger
Or disease
And there she lay?

And then in these forgotten woods
I see a sign, a trace
Left by the human clan
And what I call my race.
I mistook for matted vine
Some wire shaped like a palm,
Outstretched and rising
From a twisted base,
Asking to be found,
Embraced.

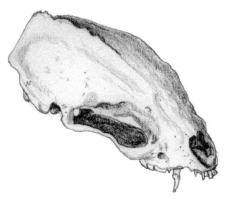

Rodent Skull

It was used perhaps
By settlers
Leaving more behind:
Turquoise jars
And leaded violet glass
With ivy-carved designs.

And what frail woman
Held this cup
Now just a shard
And pastel thin,
Speaking softly of her trials
and taking care of kin?

Could her child have worn
This piece of hardened leather boot
With tiny holes intact
And run in through
The kitchen door
Where now there's just
This oven latch?

I collect these remnants
As I walk
And on returning
Spread them out
To listen to them talk.

They speak
My every clinging fear
Of powerlessness
Or loss of dreams
Or losing those held dear,

Of the seasons
Of my life
And how the world
Goes on despite
The passing by
And passing on of life.

The passing on of life!
The seed.
The casing looked
So dead
Around the reed.
But the fawn was spared,
The child matured.
And so the remnant,
The legacy endured.

I gather up my
Crusted bits of treasure
I've brought to light,
Examined,
In which I've taken pleasure.
I will return them
On another trek
To where they'll
Rest in peace
And not be kept.

I feel new hope
And have a lighter step.

Horsetail

For Ruth Slickman
Written at Leroux Creek Inn

Fish Eye

Bahama island blue
And orange
Swirl from my brush
And touch
A glistening seaweed green.

The colors rush
Together
In a globe, an eye
That gazes out between
Coral rocks,

Astonished
To look upon the face
Of its creator.

Sea Remnants

The Holidays

"My soul in stillness waits."
These Advent words
Resound within me.

I'm absorbed
In my reflection
On the Shantivanum newsletter,
No thought
Of glancing up
Until the final page.

It's then I realize
My soul in stillness waits ...
Inside the Suburban
In the parking lot
Of the discount liquor store
In Denver!

A muted jingle
Reaches me.
I notice the red pot
By the automatic door
With the sign reading
"Sharing is Caring."

Glazed eyes rush past
The bundled ringer,
Past the huddled smokers,
Past wreaths and bows
Flailing in the wind.

Shoppers brace against the gusts
Carts rattling
Over sidewalk cracks
And curbs.
Wheeling away
Their holiday spirits.

Inside my
Warm observatory
I feel stillness
Amidst the rush,
Peace amidst
The purchasing.

I hold the memory
Of Shantivanum,
Forest of Peace.
And whisper its mantra
For all to hear.

Forest of Peace

Oh, the Starry Night

Out of the black wonder
Sails a star, looming large,
Crazy-quilted, gold stitching
Weaving in and out
Of turquoise and magenta.
Crystals cluster in its center.

Gold flames stream
From the five points
To the edges of the Universe,
Then past the edges
Where only the third eye goes.

'Past the Edges

"Gone, gone
Gone beyond
Gone beyond the beyond."

Heart Sutra

Equinox

Equinox is a big word
For a magpie.
Of course, *I* can pronounce it,
But I am new
To its meanings.

This magpie
Perched on a fence post
Overlooking melting snow
With twigs crossed in its beak
Knows
It is time to build a nest.

Spring Melt-Off

Gothic Mountain

Moon Lover

The moon
On his downward arc
Slides past my window
And into my bed.

I slowly awaken
To his gentle touch,
And opening my eyes
Look into his face.

My lover
Stirs me to tenderness
In the midst
Of the night.

Standing Gourd

Hibiscus

On to a New Horizon

Weariness of winter
Snow through the high Elk Mountains
The journey begins.

Splash of turquoise sea
Coral bouganvilla flutters
Acclimatizing.

Sun dappled hammock
Rolled up jeans behind my head
Nestled in no-time.

"*Proceed as the way opens.*"

Quaker proverb

Star Valley Stream

This April Night

Clouds
Pass before the moon
Sheer as locusts' wings.

I play a peeking game of
"Now you see it,
Now you don't."

Yet the moon never moves.
It simply shines
In all of its endurance.

Yes, I am the full moon
In the April night.

Marsh Marigolds

A Spring Pond in Early Light

May the moon
Light your path.
May you love
And laugh.

Your Path

About the Author

Judy Cox, a native of the Kansas City area, now lives in Crested Butte, Colorado where she and her husband own one of the first ski lodges on the mountain, The Nordic Inn. She is co-author of *A Pioneer Workshop* and editor and publisher of *In Sunshine and in Shadow, (Personal Portraits of A.L.S., Lou Gehrig's Disease)*. Her poetry and photography have appeared in local literary journals and newspapers.